Animals Around Us

Animals of the Seashore
Animals of the Fields and Meadows
Animals of the Woods and Forests
Animals of the Ponds and Streams

Animals of the Seashore

by
Julie Becker

EMC Publishing, St. Paul, Minnesota

**with special thanks
to
Hal Hackett
and
Little Diamond Island**

Library of Congress Cataloging in Publication Data

Becker, Julie
    Animals of the seashore.

    Includes Index
    (Her Animals around us)
    SUMMARY: Text, drawings, and photographs
describe the characteristics of ten seashore
animals. Included are the spotted sandpiper,
clam and mussel, starfish, sea urchin, brown
pelican, barnacle, periwinkle and dogwinkle,
crab, seagull, and horseshoe crab.
    1. Seashore biology—Juvenile literature.
[1. Seashore biology]   I. Roth-Evenson, Maarja.
II. Title.   III. Series.
QH95.7.B37   574.909'4'6   77-8106
ISBN 0-88436-392-9

Published by EMC Publishing
180 East Sixth Street
St. Paul, Minnesota 55101
Printed in the United States of America
0 9 8 7 6 5 4 3 2

TABLE OF CONTENTS

The Seashore

The seashore is where the land meets the sea. The waves roll on to the sand and over the rocks. There is the smell of salt in the air. Seagulls fly above the water and you can hear their loud cries.

There are high tides and low tides on the seashore. The moon and the sun pull on the water to make the tides. At high tide, the water will come in and cover the sand and the rocks. At low tide, the water will go out. A lot of little seashore animals hide under the rocks at low tide.

Many animals live on the seashore. Some fly in the air. Some dig in the sand. Some swim in the water. Some crawl on the rocks. And some hide in the seaweed.

Seashore animals are not always easy to find. Let's hunt for just a few.

The Spotted Sandpiper

The sandpiper waits. He waits for the tide to go out. He waits for the sea water to move away from the shore.

When the tide is low, the sandpiper runs out. He runs out on the wet sand. He runs on the wet sand and hunts for food.

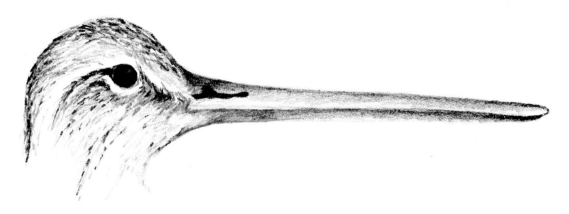

The sandpiper has a long thin bill. He digs in the sand with his long thin bill. He digs for worms and bugs and other little bits of food.

The sandpiper knows how to swim. But most of the time, he likes to run. Sometimes he runs into the shallow water. He catches little fish in the water. He catches little sea animals.

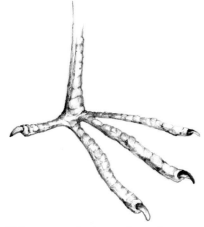

The sandpiper has long thin legs. He has four long toes on each foot. His four long toes help him to stand up on the wet sand. His four toes spread out so he will not fall over.

The spotted sandpiper likes to rock back and forth. He rocks back and forth when he hunts for food. His tail will go up. Then his tail will go down. He looks like he is on a seesaw.

The spotted sandpiper is a little bird. He has brown and white feathers. He has spots. He rocks back and forth. Keep your eyes open. Someday, you may see a spotted sandpiper running fast along the seashore.

The Clam and the Mussel

The beach is covered with shells. Some shells are white. Some shells are brown. Other shells are purple. Once upon a time, an animal lived inside each shell.

Some shells come in pairs. They are held together like two covers on a book. Clam shells come in pairs. When a clam is alive, she has two shells. Her two shells are held together on one side.

Clams like to live in sand or mud. All clams have one foot. All clams have a neck. Some clams have long necks. Other clams have little necks. Some clams have soft shells that crumble. Other clams have very hard shells.

A soft-shell clam likes to dig in the sand. She opens her shells a little bit. Her foot comes out of one end. She digs in the sand with her foot. She digs down deep.

A soft-shell clam has a long neck. When she opens her shells, she can make her neck come out too. Her foot comes out of one end. Her neck comes out of the other end.

When the tide is high, the sea water comes in. The sea water covers the sand. Clams like to eat when the tide is high.

At high tide, the clam will push her neck up. She will push her neck out of the sand. Water will cover the tip of her neck. She will eat tiny plants and animals that are in the water.

The clam has two tubes in her neck. Water runs *in* one tube. Water runs *out* of the other tube. The water brings food to the clam's mouth. She will eat the tiny plants and animals in the water. Then she will push the water out.

A mussel looks very much like a clam. Mussel shells come in pairs too. When a mussel is alive, he has two shells.

A mussel has one foot just like a clam. But a mussel will not dig in the sand. Mussels like to live on rocks.

When a mussel is young, he moves on his foot. He finds a rock. He ties thin strings to the rock. The thin strings come from his foot.

Waves rush over the rocks. But the mussel will not fall off. His thin strings will hold him on.

When a mussel wants to eat, he opens up his shells. But he will not stick his neck into the water.

The mussel lets the sea water go right between his shells. The sea water runs into a tube. Then the water will pass a bunch of tiny hairs. The tiny hairs will catch little bits of food in the water. Then the water will run out. It will run out of another tube.

Both clams and mussels can open and close their shells. They will close their shells when they are afraid. They will close their shells when they are asleep.

If you go to the seashore, dig in the wet sand. You may find a clam. Look in the water. You may find a mussel.

Try to find clam shells and mussel shells on the beach. Pick some shells up. Take them home!

The Starfish

You know that there are stars in the sky. But did you know that there were stars in the sea too?

If you go to the seashore, you may see a lot of stars in the water. The stars in the water are starfish.

If you go to a place that has starfish, you will see a lot of colors in the water. Starfish can be green, purple or orange. They can be red, brown or yellow too.

Starfish are not real fish. Real fish have backbones. Starfish do *not* have backbones. Real fish do not have arms. Starfish *do* have arms.

A lot of starfish that you see have five arms. But some starfish have ten arms and some starfish have 50 arms!

If a starfish's arm is cut off, she will grow a new one. If a starfish is cut in two, she will still live. There will be two starfish, not just one. Each starfish will grow some new arms.

A starfish has a lot of little feet on the bottom of each arm. Each foot looks like a little pipe or tube. The starfish walks on rocks with all her little tube feet. The tube feet stick to the rocks.

A starfish has a little hole on top of her body. The hole looks like this: Water runs into the hole and into the five arms. It runs into all the tube feet too. The water helps the starfish walk with all her tube feet.

If you pick up a starfish, you can see a little spot at the end of each arm. This spot is an eye. If a starfish has five arms, she will have five eyes. If she has ten arms, she will have ten eyes. A starfish can not see very well with all her eyes. She can only see light.

A starfish likes to eat clams. When a starfish wants to eat, she will get on top of a clam. A clam has two shells. The starfish will pull on the two shells with her tube feet. She will pull the two shells apart. Then she will do a funny thing.

A starfish has a mouth on the bottom of her body. She will make her stomach go out of her mouth and into the clam. Her stomach will go right to her food. That is how she eats!

If you go down to the seashore, maybe you will be lucky. Maybe you will get to see a starfish eating her dinner!

The Sea Urchin

When the tide is low, the sea water moves out. Many rocks get dry. Small pools of water are left behind. These pools of water are called tide pools. Sometimes sea urchins are found in tide pools.

A sea urchin is a round animal. His shell is full of spines. His spines feel like pine needles. They help to keep him safe.

A sea urchin can make his spines move. His spines can move up and down. They can move from side to side.

A sea urchin has a lot of little tube feet. His tube feet stick to the rocks. He can walk with his tube feet just like a starfish.

A sea urchin has tube feet on *top* of his shell too. The tube feet on top help him to move. They help him to turn over. They help him pick up food.

The sea urchin has something else on top of his shell too. He has a lot of little jaws. The jaws are on short little stalks. Two little jaws are at the end of each stalk. The little jaws look like little bird beaks.

These jaw-stalks are very hard to see. They are shorter than the spines or the tube feet. They are very very small.

The sea urchin uses his small jaw-stalks for cleaning. Sometimes little bits of rock or seaweed fall between his spines. The sea urchin picks off these little bits with his jaw-stalks.

The sea urchin is a shy animal. He likes to hide under rocks. He likes to cover up.

If the sea urchin is out in the open, he is afraid. He will catch little bits of seaweed with his jaw-stalks or his tube feet. He will put these little bits of seaweed on top of his shell. Then he can hide.

The sea urchin eats his food right off of the rocks. The sea urchin likes to eat vegetables. He likes to eat seaweed.

The sea urchin has a mouth on the bottom of his shell. He has five teeth in his mouth. He pulls little plants off the rocks with his five teeth.

Walk down to the shore when the tide is very low. Look in a tide pool. Turn over a few rocks and stones. Hunt for a sea urchin.

You may find a green sea urchin or a purple sea urchin. And if you look very carefully, you may see the shape of a star on top of his shell.

The
Brown
Pelican

A pelican is a funny bird with a crooked neck. She likes to go fishing. A pelican has no fishing pole. She likes to go fishing with her pouch.

A pelican's fishing pouch is on her bill. Her bill is very long. It is almost as long as her crooked neck.

The pelican's pouch is at the bottom of her long bill. The pouch hangs down. It is made of thick skin. It can hold water. It can hold fish.

When a pelican wants to catch a fish, she stands up on the water. She flaps her long wings fast. She takes off. She begins to fly. She flies up high into the air.

When the pelican gets up high, she will hardly move her wings. She will float on the air waves. She will look down at the water. She will look for a flash of white or a flash of silver. She will look for fish.

When the pelican sees a fish, she will dive down. She will dive down fast. When she gets near the water, she will stop her dive. She will do a belly flop. She will make a big splash. She will stick her pouch into the water and she will scoop up a fish.

When the pelican scoops up a fish, she gets water in her pouch. She lets the water go out of her pouch. Then she holds her head back and she swallows the fish.

Some people think that a pelican can fly when her pouch is full of fish. But this is not true. A pelican can not fly when her pouch is full. She swallows her food before she flies.

A pelican can dive, but she will not go under the water. She will always stay on top. She has little bags of air under her skin. The little air bags help her to float. She can not sink.

When the pelican wants to lay eggs, she makes a nest. She makes a nest in the top of a tree. She makes her nest out of sticks and grass and weeds.

She lays three eggs in her nest. When the eggs hatch, the baby pelicans come out. The baby pelicans do not look pretty. They do not have feathers. They have dark red skin. Their eyes are not open.

When the babies get bigger, they grow white fuzzy feathers. They begin to eat a lot. They begin to eat fish. Each baby will eat four pounds of fish a day.

The mother pelican hunts for their food. Each time she gets a fish, she will swallow it part way. After she swallows a lot of fish, she will go back to her babies.

When she gets back to the nest, she feeds her babies. First she spits up some of the fish. She spits up the fish into her pouch. Then her babies stick their bills right into her pouch. They eat all the fish.

Pelicans may look funny to you. They have long bills. They have crooked necks. They have big floppy feet. But they can do a lot of things. They can swim and fly and dive and fish.

You may like to fish in the sea too. But you will never be able to fish as well as the pelican can!

The Barnacle

Millions of baby barnacles are swimming in the sea. They are riding the waves. They are looking for a place to live.

Each baby barnacle wants to find a rock. He wants to find a rock where he can live for the rest of his life. Every day, he swims around. He hunts for a place to live.

One day, he finds a rock. He begins to make his home. He makes some sticky stuff. The sticky stuff is on the back of his head. His head sticks to the side of the rock. Then he grows a hard white shell. This hard white shell keeps him safe.

31

There are four small shells on top of the hard white shell. These four small shells make a door. The barnacle can open and close his door when he wants to eat.

The barnacle eats in a funny way. His head is stuck to the rock. He lies on his back. He has a bunch of hairy legs. His legs look like little feathers. When the barnacle wants to eat, he opens up his door. He waves his hairy feather-legs around in the water.

The sea water is full of tiny plants and animals. The barnacle picks up some of these tiny plants and animals with his feather-legs. He sweeps this food right into his mouth.

When the barnacle is not eating, he brings his legs inside. He closes his door.

Sometimes the barnacle must close his door very tightly. He has to keep wet inside or he will die. At low tide, the water moves away from the rocky shore. The barnacle may not be covered with water. That is why he has to close his door so tightly.

At high tide, the sea water will come back. The barnacle will be safe. He can open up his door once again. He will not dry out.

When this barnacle was a baby, he found a place to live. He was lucky. Millions of baby barnacles die before they ever find a home.

It is hard to find a place to live. It is hard to find a space on the rocks. Sometimes hundreds and hundreds of barnacles live on just one rock. There is no room for one more barnacle.

Go down to the shore. Look for barnacles that live on the rocks. Find some barnacles that are eating. Watch the feather-legs. Watch them wave around in the water. Watch the barnacles kick food into their mouths!

The Periwinkle and the Dogwinkle

If you walk on the rocks along the shore, you can find hundreds and hundreds of snails. There are snails on top of rocks. There are snails under the rocks. There are snails hiding in the seaweed.

All snails have just one foot. A snail's foot is flat. It is very strong. It is full of muscles.

A periwinkle is a snail. He lives very close to the shore. He likes to move around on the rocks. He moves around on his one flat foot.

The periwinkle hunts for food on the rocks. He likes to eat plants. He likes to eat seaweed.

The periwinkle has a strange mouth. He has a strange tongue. His tongue is full of teeth. He scrapes the rocks with his teeth. He scrapes little plants off of the rocks.

The periwinkle stays on rocks that are close to shore. When the tide is high, the periwinkle is under the water. But when the tide is low, the sea water moves out. The periwinkle may be left on a dry rock.

The periwinkle has to stay wet inside or he will die. He has a round hard circle at the end of his foot. This round hard circle makes a door. When the tide is very low, the periwinkle will close his door. He will close his door very tightly. Then he will not dry out.

A dogwinkle is another kind of snail. A dogwinkle and a periwinkle do not look the same. A periwinkle has a smooth shell. A dogwinkle's shell is not smooth.

A dogwinkle will not stay on just one rock. She likes to move around. She likes to hunt for food. A dogwinkle likes to eat meat. She likes to eat barnacles.

A dogwinkle has a long tongue in her mouth. Her tongue is full of teeth. Her tongue is very strong.

When the dogwinkle wants to eat, she finds a barnacle. The barnacle's shell has a crack. The dogwinkle sticks her tongue into the crack. Her tongue and her teeth go inside of the barnacle's shell. After the dogwinkle eats, the barnacle's shell is empty.

If you look at a dogwinkle eating her dinner, you can see her head. There are two stalks on top of her head. She can move her stalks. One eye is at the end of each stalk.

A dogwinkle likes to lay her eggs under a rock. Her eggs are long and yellow. They feel like rubber. They stand up. If you pop a dogwinkle's egg, water runs out. This water smells. Some people think the water smells like dead fish.

If you go to the rocks at low tide, you will see a lot of periwinkles and dogwinkles. Watch them move. Watch them eat. See if you can find a row of dogwinkle eggs under a rock.

The Crab

Many crabs live on the
seashore. Some hide under
rocks and some dig in the sand.
Others swim in the sea.

Crabs come in many colors.
They can be orange or green or
brown.

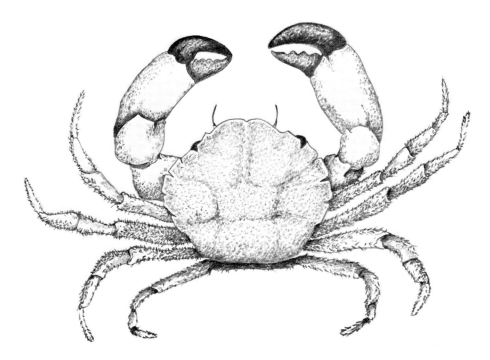

All crabs have ten legs. The two legs in front have claws. A crab can catch things with his claws. He can rip food with his claws.

A crab will eat almost anything. He will eat dead clams and dead fish. He will eat worms. He will eat little plants and animals in the water.

Sometimes a green crab sees a clam neck sticking up in the sand. He will run over to the clam neck. He will cut off the neck with one of his claws. He will eat the clam neck and the clam will die.

A crab has a very busy mouth. He has a lot of mouth parts. The mouth parts are very sharp. He can rip food with his mouth parts. He can bite food. He can crush food.

A crab's mouth parts move a lot. Sometimes a crab blows bubbles in his mouth.

A crab needs oxygen to live. He gets his oxygen from the water. Water runs into cracks around his legs. When the water gets inside of his shell, it runs into his gills. His gills take oxygen from the water. Then the water runs out of the crab's mouth. That is why a crab blows bubbles.

A crab has lollipop eyes. Each eye sits on top of a stalk. The crab can move his eye stalks all around. He can see very well. He can see shapes. He can see colors. He can see plants and animals moving in the water.

A crab runs sideways. He runs sideways when he wants to get some food. He runs sideways when he is afraid. He runs sideways when he wants to hide.

There are many kinds of crabs in the sea. Some crabs are good swimmers. Other crabs are good walkers.

A blue crab is a swimming crab. A blue crab has back legs that are flat. They look like little paddles. The little paddles help the blue crab to swim.

A rock crab lives near the shore. He walks under the water. He walks in the sand and on the rocks. His back legs have points at the end. These pointed legs are good for walking.

Sometimes a crab hurts one of his legs. He hurts his leg badly and his leg comes off. If this happens, he can grow a new leg. He grows a new leg when he gets a new shell.

When a crab grows bigger, his old shell is too small for him. He needs a new shell. The back of his old shell will crack. He will come out of his old shell. He will molt.

After the crab backs out of his old shell, he is very soft. He is very weak. He can not eat. He has to hide. He will hide under a rock. He will wait for his new shell to get hard.

All crabs molt. Blue crabs molt and rock crabs molt. Green crabs molt too.

The seashore is full of crabs. Look under a few rocks. Lift up some seaweed. You may find a crab's secret hiding place.

The Seagull

Seagulls are almost always around the seashore. You can see them sitting on the rocks. You can see them flying over the boats. You can hear them screaming in the air.

Seagulls are gray and white. They have sharp yellow beaks. Their feet have webs. They have long wings.

Seagulls look beautiful when they fly. They beat their long wings up and down. They ride on the air. They glide.

Seagulls like to eat fish. They like to follow fishing boats. They glide behind a fishing boat. They glide on the air. Their wings hardly move. They wait for bits of food. If a fisherman throws out a fish, a seagull will catch it in the air.

A seagull will eat fish. A seagull will eat worms. She will eat dead snails or dead clams. She will eat eggs. She will even eat garbage! She will fly over a garbage dump and hunt for left-over food.

Sometimes a seagull can not find garbage. Then she will hunt for food along the seashore. She likes to eat crab meat. She will fly down to the shore and catch a crab. She will catch him with her sharp beak.

Then the seagull will do something strange. She will hold the crab in her beak. She will fly up high in the air. She will fly over the rocks. Then she will drop the crab on the rocks. When the crab hits the rocks, his shell will crack.

After the seagull drops the crab, she flies back down to the rocks. She has very good eyes. She can see the broken shell. She lands on the rocks and eats the fresh crab meat.

48

The seagull makes a nest in the spring. She makes her nest out of grass, sticks and seaweed. She makes it on the ground.

A seagull will lay three eggs in her nest. Her eggs will be brown. They will have black spots on them. Both the mother seagull and the father seagull will take turns sitting on the eggs. They will keep the eggs warm.

The eggs will hatch in about 30 days. The mother and father will take care of their babies. They will feed their babies.

A baby seagull is not gray and white. A baby seagull is brown. She has spots on her feathers. She has a black beak.

When a young seagull is just seven days old, she will learn how to swim. When she is 20 days old, she will learn how to fly. When she is two months old, she will take care of herself. She will hunt for food along the seashore. She will fly with the rest of the seagulls over the water and over the rocks.

The Horseshoe Crab

Horseshoe crabs are the oldest kind of animal on Earth. Horseshoe crabs have been living on Earth for over 500 million years. Horseshoe crabs were on Earth before dinosaurs!

A horseshoe crab looks very strange. She has a hard brown shell. The front of her shell looks like a horseshoe.

You do not need to be afraid of a horseshoe crab. She will not hurt you. If you find a horseshoe crab in the sand or in the mud, pick her up. Turn her over.

A horseshoe crab has a lot of legs. The two little legs on top are not real legs. They are just little claws. The horseshoe crab will pick up food with her little claws. She can not walk on them.

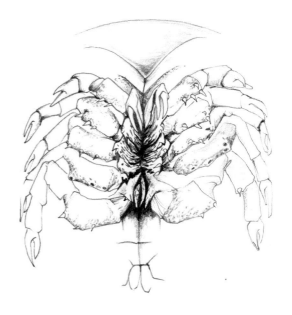

A horseshoe crab has ten real legs. She has five legs on each side. The first four pairs of legs have claws. The horseshoe crab can walk on these legs.

The last pair of legs are not like the others. They have four spines at the end. The spines are flat. The horseshoe crab can push with her flat spines. She can push in the mud. The horseshoe crab can clean with her flat spines too. She can clean her gills and her flaps.

Her gills are under her legs. Flaps cover up her gills. The flaps look like brown playing cards. She has six pairs of flaps. Each pair of flaps covers up one pair of gills.

The horseshoe crab uses her gills to get oxygen. When she wants oxygen, she opens her flaps.

The horseshoe crab can move her flaps a lot. She can fan them back and forth. Her flaps help her to swim.

The horseshoe crab likes to swim upside down. She starts to swim right-side up. Then she turns a back flip. She turns upside down. She fans her flaps. She moves her legs. She looks like a small round boat in the water.

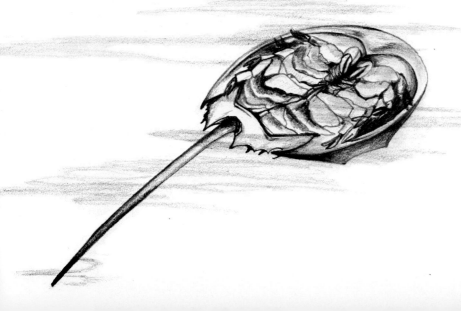

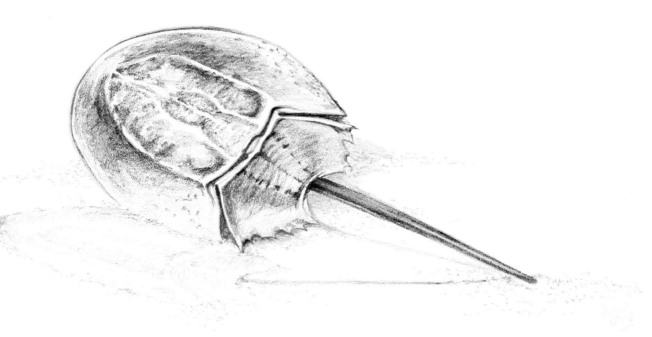

The horseshoe crab has a long tail. The tail has a point at the end. Her tail can be a big help.

Sometimes she lands on her back. She wants to turn over. She pokes her tail in the sand. Her tail will help her turn over. Then she will be on her feet.

The horseshoe crab hunts for food in the sand. She walks on the sand. She looks for worms or soft-shell clams.

No other animal in the world eats like a horseshoe crab. The horseshoe crab picks up food with her claws. Then she puts her food on her shoulders.

Her shoulders are next to her legs. They are full of short spines. They work like a garbage truck. They grind up the food. Then they roll it into her mouth.

Sometimes little bits of sand or clam shells go into her mouth. The horseshoe crab spits these things out after she eats her dinner.

If the horseshoe crab eats a lot of food, she will grow. When it is time for her to grow, she will need a new shell. She will molt. She will swallow a lot of water. The front part of her shell will crack open. Then she will dig down in the sand.

When she is safe, she will crawl out of her old shell. Then she will grow. Her new shell is very soft. It will get hard in about 24 hours.

A horseshoe crab molts. A blue crab molts. A rock crab molts too. But a horseshoe crab is *not* a real crab.

Real crabs do not have tails. Real crabs do not grind up food with their shoulders. Real crabs do not have brown flaps. Real crabs do not swim upside down.

If you find a horseshoe crab on the beach, take care. Remember, you are looking at the oldest kind of animal in the whole wide world!

CREDITS

Designed by Gale William Ikola and Cyril John Schlosser
Illustrated by Maarja Roth-Evenson

Photo Credits

INDEX